How to Start Your Own YouTube Network:

An Insider's Guide

By
Carey Martell

How to Start Your Own YouTube Network: An Insider's Guide
Copyright 2016

ISBN 13: 978-1532959363
ISBN 10: 1532959362

Published by Martell Books
http://martellbooks.com/

For information regarding special discounts for bulk purchases, please contact Martell Books via the contact form on our website.

"When you're young, you look at television and think, there's a conspiracy. The networks have conspired to dumb us down. But when you get a little older, you realize that's not true. The networks are in business to give people exactly what they want."

-Steve Jobs

TABLE OF CONTENTS

Who This Book is For

First off, if you are looking for a book that will give you advice on how to shoot and edit videos for YouTube, this book will not help you. There's many books like that on the market already and I suggest you read one of those.

This book is purely about the business aspect of starting a YouTube multi-channel network, otherwise known as a "YouTube MCN".

It became clear to me that there is a need in the market for book that explains the business of a YouTube MCN. I think this is a book that needs to be written, and there are very few people who possess the necessary knowledge and experience to write such a book.

As the founder of two YouTube MCNs I believe myself to be certainly among the candidates. However, given that I started my MCN with no money, grew it to tens of millions of views and thousands of partners then sold it for over a hundred thousand times what I had invested into the business, I consider myself to be uniquely qualified to write this book in a way no one else could.

So, to answer the question about who this book is for,

- This book is for those entrepreneurs who desire to start their own MCN and need a guidebook.

- This book is also for those YouTube creators who want to better understand the business they are involved in.

- It is also for those YouTube employees looking for answers in how, despite its extreme popularity, the platform has not reached the degree of profitability that more traditional entertainment companies currently have, and how working better with MCNs might address this gap.

- It is yet also for those traditional entertainment business executives who are woefully ignorant about the business of web television and need someone to bring them up to date.

As a prerequisite you should be familiar with the information in my book *The Lean Channel: YouTube for Entrepreneurs (* *http://amzn.to/1XBa0ux* *)*. It covers a lot of basic information about building a business on YouTube that I will not be repeating in this book.

Also, I won't be discussing topics beyond the initial startup phase of the network. This is because there are numerous ways you can scale a network depending on your goals and the kind of content it specializes in, and if I tried to cover every possible scenario I think I would never finish writing this book.

Ultimately this book is what you get out of it. I hope you find it useful.

Carey Martell
April, 26th 2016

http://careymartell.com/

Why Start a YouTube network?

If you're considering becoming a well-known behemoth in online broadcasting, right now the cheapest way to do so is by starting a YouTube network.

The core advantage of using YouTube to build your online broadcasting network is because your startup does not need to pay for its own video streaming server space, tech support, software updates or even acquire its own advertisers initially. YouTube will provide all of these services in exchange for 49% of the ad revenue your network generates. Until you reach a very high viewership level (we're talking billions of monthly views here), it is very economical to allow YouTube to handle these aspects of the business.

YouTube's platform also has features for closed captions, allowing subtitles for different languages to be easily implemented. YouTube also supports other features 3D television and 360 video. All of this means operating YouTube Network is a low-cost entry point to creating a HD television network on the web that is both reliable, profitable and has access to all the latest video related technologies.

Furthermore, rather than need to produce your own original content, you'll be better served by offering consultancy to help existing YouTube channel owners at first, and recruit them into your network. Over time you'll grow your distribution channel and mailing lists, and be able to create a genuine online broadcast network that can exist off YouTube's platform.

Now, while it is cheaper to start a YouTube network this does not mean it requires less business development work. There are many necessary steps you must take to generate the right brand and presence within the market, and providing reliable advice to creators will help all starting networks build relationships in positive ways that can't be purchase from the onset.

However, if you don't know much about YouTube or the business aspect of the industry, from whence can you learn this information? So where do you begin?

Lucky you for finding this book. I've successfully started a YouTube network with very little money and grew it to where it was acquired by a traditional film studio. Then I grew another network, using the significant capital resources the studio had available. I have a very unique perspective on the business as a result, which is probably unlike that of any other MCN founder.

In this guide I will teach you pretty much everything you need to know in order to build your own network, and I'll be frank in my advice, too. I don't think there is another book like this on the market right now, but I think it's needed for a few reasons.

1. People who want to create YouTube networks have no resources to guide them on how to build one.
2. People reach out to me all the time for consultancy on how to start an MCN. Not all of them can pay my $150 an hour rate for my laser-focused attention on their startup. Yet, I do want to help them and this book is the next best thing to hiring me as a consultant.
3. YouTube creators have no source of information about the operation of a YouTube network that isn't produced by a bias source. Not knowing for sure if something is true or not, with no neutral third party's perspective, often leads to mistrust.

I built my network, sold it and have moved on. I don't have much of a desire to start another one, so consider this book the most unbiased, frankly truthful perspective you're likely to ever read on the subject.

Furthermore, I don't really care what bridges I burn by saying what I write here, or what competitors I create, because I'm not looking to start any future MCNs. I have no horse in this race anymore (and how glorious it is to be able to say that!).

This book is written out of a genuine desire to provide information for those that want to understand how a YouTube network operates and how to build one yourself if you so desire. That's precisely what you'll get here.

Why I Started a YouTube Network

I think the reasons behind why anyone starts a certain business gives great insight into how they view the purpose of that business. I believe it would be difficult for you to fully comprehend my reasoning behind the advice I give in this book if you don't understand why I got into this business in the first place.

As a child I was largely a loner. Though I had some natural leadership ability which expressed itself when necessary, I spent most of my grade school years without any deep bonds of friendship. This was not due to lack of trying, but rather I think because of the intellectual gaps between my child self and other kids my own age. In the third grade my concerned teachers had my intellect tested which revealed I ranked relatively high on the intelligence quotient; I still recall an astonished teacher explaining to me that I had a high school level of reading comprehension and writing composition -- and these talents coupled with my excellent memory afforded me an above average ability to learn visually. I've found these to be useful talents for a loner.

My intelligence ranking was such that my school actually started receiving extra funds from the state which were meant to fund my involvement in extracurricular activities, which were supposed to be designed to cultivate my natural talents; however due to various circumstances which for now are very private to my life, it was decided by the school faculty that the state's money would be spent on weekly purchases of comic books for me to read. Though this may sound peculiar and there was undoubtedly better use of the funds, it turned out an investment into comic books would not be wasteful.

Story-telling was and continues to be my first passion. I lived vicariously through reading stories, both fiction and biographical. Before I had advanced to middle school I had read every book that the grade school library possessed, which forced me to often sneak across the street to the city library during my recess hours. My thirst for knowledge was unquenchable, and for others this was annoyingly so. My father would often take me to the local gun shows where he would have a table as a dealer, and I would spend most of the weekend at the tables of other merchants who sold books -- speed reading through military manuals, martial art books and various other Paladin Press titles to ingest as much information as possible before the merchant could chase me off.

Fantasy is my favourite genre of fiction and I gained the habit of reading several chapters of a good heroic story every night before bed. Whether it was *The Chronicles of Narnia* or Arthurian romances I went to sleep dreaming of adventure. This spurred a natural interest in fantasy television and films, and this fascination translated into a desire to one-day write and direct such films.

Somewhere among the boxes in my storage unit are the notepads I filled with stories I wrote as a child; though they are written nowhere near the sophistication I now possess, they harken me back to my earliest dreams for the future. It is the characters I created, existing only in the words I strung down into paper that kept me comforted in times of stress and sorrow.

It was my desire to break into the entertainment business that led me to first write comic books. By this time, I had received an honourable discharged from the military and was looking to finally pursue my passion. However, I lacked confidence in my writing ability, so I worked with an artist to create my first published work, *Deathfist Ninja GKaiser,* as a comic. As I worked on the comic I took a day job as a private security officer at a steel plant.

I will openly admit it is hard for me to do occupations that are non-challenging to my intellect and skill-set. Sitting in a booth or a car staring at the night is a frustrating experience; for hours I dwelled on the thought that my life had more meaning than this and that I was wasting my potential. Each passing second felt like part of my soul was dying. I knew deeply in my bones that I was meant for something else. The only way I was able to endure working as a security guard was by spending the long nights with my laptop, writing new scripts and notes on comic art in between my patrol shifts.

Sadly, the arrangement between the comic artist and myself fleeted out as I ran out of money to fund the venture. Self-publishing in print, I discovered, was an expensive endeavour and I had no luck as a door to door salesman, trying to convince comic stores to pick the title up. I spent $5,000 of my military savings with nothing to show for it but boxes of unsold comic books. This failure led me to hone an earlier work, a short novel I had written in my spare time while deployed during Operation Iraqi Freedom. This story was a fantasy about a boy who becomes possessed by the ghost of a demon king and it explores deep ideas about the nature of good and evil. I was proud of the uniqueness of story and thought it would be well enjoyed by children.

Eventually, after a fruitless three years of attempting to sell the book to a publisher I opted to self-publish it through Amazon's Kindle platform as *Pandemonia Chronicles* (http://amzn.to/1lsELuK). Despite not becoming a best-seller as I dreamed it would, it has at least has been reviewed very positively by those who have read it.

Anyway, during the time my manuscript for *Pandemonia* was getting rejected from publishers I gave YouTube a serious consideration as an outlet for re-telling the *GKaiser* story.

I also worked briefly as a video game designer, and then a journalist. As a game designer I designed large parts of the combat mechanics and wrote a lot of quest flavour text for an expansion for the game *Nexus: The Kingdom of the Winds*, but as this was freelance work for a small publisher I was not compensated well for it. I had hoped that by demonstrating my skills and work ethic it would turn into a full time position but after being informed they were not hiring any new positions I ended the relationship.

My work as a game journalist was equally disappointing; despite regularly producing game review articles and investing a lot of time into networking at conventions and electronic trade shows I was still only getting "compensated" through exposure of my work while the websites themselves retained 100% of the ad revenue money.

Learning from my failure with prior attempts to sell my stories I approached my YouTube channel differently; for the outcome to be different I would need to master the craft of marketing and branding. After a lot of missteps and grave blunders, I was able to grow the channel to millions of video views and over 14,000 channel subscribers. While this sounded impressive, given that YouTube ad revenue only pays $2 for every 1,000 video watches I did not make a lot of money. Ultimately I came to the realization that I lacked the necessary talents to be Talent in front of a camera. It was a sober day when I realized I would not be attracting the millions of subscribers necessary to earn a living from the channel.

My experiences failing to get published and secure a position at a game publisher also taught me that my unique skills as a writer and designer were unappreciated by management at most companies; even when work was available in the freelance market it was often very low pay considering the enormous scope of work required of the tasks. While there are companies who do appreciate these skills and compensate appropriately, I lacked the necessary job experience to be competitive for these limited number of coveted positions.

However, the techniques and tricks I learned were valuable to someone; YouTube creators. It was this realization that led me to figure out if I applied these same techniques to a better product, the effects would be better. My path then became clear; I would become an executive in the entertainment industry focused on catering to the new media world, and this would be the best use my true talents.

Starting my own YouTube network led me to obtain my first real success in the market. Using low-cost internet marketing techniques such as email lists, search engine optimization and video sales pitches, I quickly grew the Power Up TV network to millions of video views and subscribers by recruiting creators who fit a narrowly defined customer profile. I then sold the network fourteen months later for over a hundred thousand times what it cost me to build the startup while simultaneously securing a top executive position at a large movie studio. During my tenure as vice president of the television division my life-long attraction to visual storytelling came into full-force; I was comfortably able to review the quality of submitted screenplays and I am quite proud of the quality of the finished projects I selected for green-lighting.

It is my belief that, although my life has been filled with challenges which often ended in failure, because I learned from my mistakes my life has stayed on the correct course of action. My original goal was to share my love of stories with other people and this goal led me to develop a YouTube network, as a network is a fantastic way to help people tell their stories.

I like to think my experience is not unique and there is someone else out there reading these words right now, who is about to use the knowledge in this book to embark on their own great adventure in digital video.

Why Are YouTube Networks Important?

In my past as a network executive I found it routine to need to explain how a YouTube network fits into the ecosystem of online video and provides a valuable service for both YouTube and the creators who join these networks. The answers I have always given are thus;

1. Google is not fond of giving free customer support for its products. YouTube is no exception. Google likes YouTube Networks because we can provide the bulk of customer support to our clients and only email YouTube's team about things they absolutely need to deal with.

2. The content contributors (the YouTube Partners) like having a live employee to talk to via Facebook, Skype and email. They realize they need a partner to help them market their videos so they can focus solely on video production. They also need help acquiring sponsors for their shows.

3. Google also likes that YouTube Networks can develop original shows that make AdWords more valuable, without Google needing to invest its own money into developing those shows. YouTube will often invest into select channels and programs, but it does not need to do this at the same scale a traditional network does because there are so so many hundreds of thousands of creators out there producing original content with the assistance of YouTube networks.

YouTube Networks as a "Next-Gen" Television Network

Some people have asked me if YouTube multi-channel networks are the "next generation" of television networks. I think they are, for the following three reasons:

1. MCNs fulfils the needs of Millennials who are Talent, Crew or Audience.
   - Personal development: offering resources and education in how to produce content.
   - Cause-focused: MCNs often includes cause-focused content in their libraries and endorse creators who take part in social movements.
   - Authenticity: talent can be themselves and build a brand around their "realness" within a niche community.

2. MCNs leverages new technologies to enhance traditional business practices.
   - Strong multi-screen focus; content is available for viewing on any device, anywhere in the world.
   - Interactive media (in-app purchases, surveys, voting) are a staple of the business model
   - Crowdfunding is used to reduce and/or eliminate risk involved in the development process by building massive audience demand for a show when it is still in the idea stage, and even gaining production funds to help reduce final costs.
   - Strong emphasis in using analytics to identify laser-focused niche audiences that can be sold to advertisers.

3. MCNs operate as a "factory" of profitable content production and sales.

- They keep a stable of talent and crew with the network, often playing match-maker to build audiences for this talent.
- MCNs are a modernized version of the "Golden Age" studio star-system of old Hollywood.
- The network often acts as both a studio and a talent agency.
- They utilize a broadcast monetization model focused on advertising, with subscriptions for premium content.

How does a YouTube network make money?

One of the most common questions I have been asked by those new to the concept of YouTube networks is how they earn money. The answer is multi-folded, as there are usually several revenue streams at play with the operation of any network.

The four main methods are;

1. Content contributors (called YouTube Partners) give a portion of their ad-revenue (15-40%) to the network in exchange for access to the network's tech support, promotion and unlocking of YT channel features. They typically sign a two-year contract with the network.

2. The network can also manage the content contributor's social media pages (FB, Twitter, etc.) giving the network incredibly reach for paid advertisements.

3. Sponsors can pay the network to embed ads into videos, or request product reviews from the content contributors. Because the network can have hundreds of content contributors, the reach obtained through the network can be quite substantial, delivering hundreds of thousands of visits to targeted websites.

4. The network can develop original IP video programming to later sell merchandise licenses to manufacturers.

Outside of the primary four revenue streams, there are also secondary types which apply to specific networks;

1. Clients with large libraries of content can pay the network to manage their assets on YouTube, allowing the network to SEO (search engine optimize) and manage the online audiences for the client.

2. Original IP Shows can be developed that collaborate with local businesses, such as "reality TV shows".

3.   The network can move into ebook publishing to develop web shows based on novels to help drive ebook sales.

4.   Public domain movies and videos can be monetized and included into original IP shows, such as children's programming.

5.   The network can establish a music label, producing music videos for the artists in exchange for a split of ad revenue and digital download sales.

6.   Apps can be developed that drive up user engagement and make it easier to discover the network's videos. Apps themselves can have advertisements in them or paid subscriptions.

These are just a sample of the different kinds of revenue streams some networks use to scale their business, and not all will apply to every kind of network. I listed them only as an example of what is possible.

The Life Cycle of a YouTube Network

Most YouTube networks have a very predictable life-cycle. This is because, like any business, there are specific phases it must undergo in order to succeed in the market and then scale to obtain more customers and consequently generate more revenue.

The best way I can explain the life-cycle for a YouTube multi-channel is with the following graph.

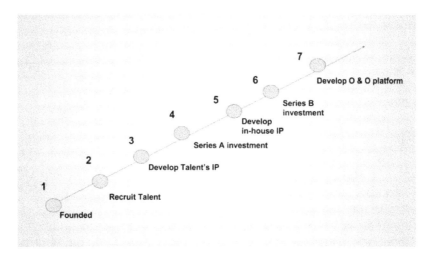

YouTube networks essentially have seven stages in the startup phase of their life. These are;

Founded: This is the date the network is formally drawn up and strategized by its founder(s). Like any startup this is the period the company defines its core values, branding and what kind of services it will offer to customers. For a network this means the founders decide what kind of content it will focus on distributing and what kind of services it will provide to creators when they join the network.

As with any startup I recommend new MCN founders to use lean startup methodology to build the network. This is what I did very successfully with Power Up TV.

PROBLEM	SOLUTION	UNIQUE VALUE PROPOSITION	UNFAIR ADVANTAGE	CUSTOMER SEGMENTS
1) YouTube Partners are locked into long-term contracts with networks. 2) YouTube Partners need help growing their channel subscribers. 3) YouTube Partners need help getting brand sponsorships.	1) Offer month-to-month contracts. 2) Offer an e-learning course teaching YouTubers how to be marketers. 3) Leverage connections with brands to negotiate deals for YouTubers.	"Get a FREE copy of Xsplit Broadcaster when you join our YouTube network! Up to 95% ad revenue split, no lock-in contracts. Huge free music library to use in your videos. Get free games. BONUS: Recruit channels and you'll get PAID 15% of their ad revenue!"	1) Comprehensive e-learning course written by a long-time YouTube expert (me) 2) Blog network for sharing the message. 3) Large mailing list of YouTubers.	1) YouTubers who make gaming-related videos about popular games (Minecraft, LoL, WoW, etc) 2) YouTubers who have lost trust in other MCNs due to lengthy contracts and lack of communication.
	KEY METRICS 1) Number of Partners 2) Number of video views 3) Number of subscribers to social profiles + mailing lists		**CHANNELS**	
EXISTING ALTERNATIVES Machinima Maker Studios Fullscreen		**HIGH-LEVEL CONCEPT** "An honest Machinima"		**EARLY ADOPTERS** Heavy social media users (FB groups, Twitter, reddit)

COST STRUCTURE	REVENUE STREAMS
1) Website hosting, web design software, graphics 2) Mailchimp list 3) Facebook Ads	1) AdWords Ad Revenue

This is the lean business model canvas I used when I planned Power Up TV.

Recruit Talent: This is the second phase. Here the MCN attempts to sell its services to YouTube creators and convince them to join the network. Your sales pitch will get refined during this process as you interact with creators and learn what kinds of language convince them to accept your offer. If you did your market research correctly, you should not need to change your offer to convince creators to sign up; all you need do is find the correct sales pitch for the kind of customer they are.

Recruiting talent will always occur throughout the life of your MCN, as there is a high amount of churn in most networks, but at this stage 100% of the MCN's efforts are focused on recruiting talent and growing as fast as possible.

Develop Talent's IP: During this phase an MCN has acquired a sizable amount of traction in terms of recruitment. The MCN is likely generating sufficient revenue to hire staff that exists solely to work with those creators that have joined it, and help them build their channels into brands. Every network needs a few creators who can be pointed to as stars of the network, for other creators to aspire to become. The message the MCN sends to other creators is that if you want to become as successful as Channel X in our MCN, you need to sign up and join us.

Series A Investment: By this point the MCN is looking to expand their operations beyond simply working with the contractor talent. The MCN needs a cash infusion in order to hire more staff to assist with recruitment, video promotion and talent management. The MCN likely has outgrown its current small offices (which often are ran out of the apartment of the founder) and needs to secure office space -- probably even build a few stages, too.

Develop in-house IP: Using capital from the series A investment, the MCN will start producing content it solely owns. It's at this phase of the MCN lifespan that the relationship between talent managers and creators often changes, because the MCN becomes more focused on its own content and is less interested in growing the brands of the creators who got it to this point. This isn't so much an intentional slight as a practicality of the business; the fact is the ROI for the MCN to produce its own content is much higher than that for investing into the creator's content.

The MCN will leverage its database of audiences which have been harvested from the channels in the network. The vast majority of the network promotion efforts will focus on building audiences for the in-house developed IP, and there will become less opportunities for creators in the network to obtain promotion on social media and mailing lists.

At the same time, the MCN will focus the bulk of its talent management services on assisting the top 10% most popular creators in the network and try to keep them happy in order to continue using those channels to advertise the network and entice advertisers.

Series B investment: The MCN will likely have spent most of its Series A by this point but used it to develop a few in-house properties that have become very popular on YouTube. The MCN will is likely to change up its executive board and bring in more experienced leadership.

Develop O & O platform: A good portion of the Series B investment will be used to develop an owned and operated platform so that the network can better monetize its content. YouTube will still remain host to the bulk of its content but the most premium content will only be available to audiences who watch it on the network's video streaming website and/or mobile app, usually as part of a monthly subscription.

Once a network has reached this point the vast majority of promotion efforts are focused on in-house IP and very little promotion is done for individual creator channels. This does not deter most creators from joining a network because they are unaware of the network's change in focus.

The Content Pyramid

Unlike a traditional television network whose programming largely consists of internally produced shows and licensed properties, your typical YouTube network has three layers of content which consists of what I refer to as the content pyramid.

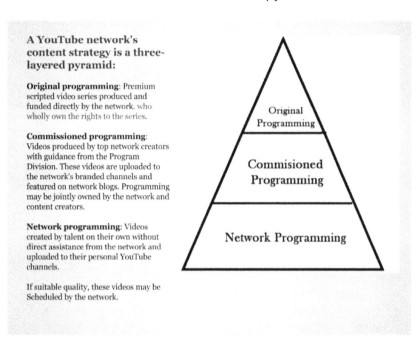

A YouTube network's content strategy is a three-layered pyramid:

Original programming: Premium scripted video series produced and funded directly by the network, who wholly own the rights to the series.

Commissioned programming: Videos produced by top network creators with guidance from the Program Division. These videos are uploaded to the network's branded channels and featured on network blogs. Programming may be jointly owned by the network and content creators.

Network programming: Videos created by talent on their own without direct assistance from the network and uploaded to their personal YouTube channels.

If suitable quality, these videos may be Scheduled by the network.

(Pyramid diagram labels, top to bottom: Original Programming / Commisioned Programming / Network Programming)

The pyramid is an abstract scale; Original programming makes up very little of a network's library, with Network programming making up the vast majority of content. Without exception, the Network programming available in the library of an MCN is in a constant state of flux as talent joins and leaves the network -- almost always, the talent owns 100% of the rights to the content they upload to their personal YouTube channels and the MCN is simply monetizing it under a non-exclusive license agreement.

Essentially, most MCNs use a business model that allows for the mass production and promotion of video content, which I refer to as the "Network Factory model".

The Network Factory model relies heavily on the constant recruitment of talent channels who will then develop, produce and release content. The MCN usually will play no direct role in the majority of the content that is produced and released on the talent channels; there are times when an MCN will provide production resources such as access to equipment and stages, or possibly even funding, but these are rare events.

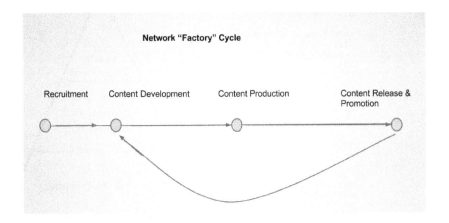

Recruitment:
Self-explanatory. The network recruits a creator into the network.

Content Development:
The creator develops an idea for content (a video) to go on their channel, usually without the involvement of the network.

Content Production:
The creator produces the video for their channel, usually without the involvement of the network.

Content release and promotion:
This stage of the cycle is where the video is released to the public and promoted to audiences in order to gain views. It often includes the following tactics when an MCN assists with this process:

1. MCNs use traditional TV scheduling practices for audience building; lead-ins, cross-programming, day-parting, promos, etc. -- some creators also do this amongst themselves.
2. Promos and pilot episodes for new shows are often uploaded to YouTube, Facebook, Vimeo, etc. as many video platforms as possible; however, full episodes of Original Programming are often only available on the O&O platform of the network, where monetization can be maximized through subscriptions.
3. The Talent and Crew leverage their personal tribes to promote the release schedule.
4. The MCN leverages mailing lists, social profiles, blog network and third-party media relations (newspapers, industry influencers, etc.) to build broader awareness.

After the video has been released and promoted, a creator goes back to the Content Development Phase and the process repeats. This is the strength of the network factory model; the bulk of content is produced without the network having to invest any resources whatsoever into the development and production of the content. All the MCN needs to do is help promote the content once it is released.

What kind of content tier should your MCN focus on?

As you can see in the pyramid, your network programming represents the bulk of the videos you have at your disposal for programming.

When you first start your network you probably won't have any other types of content and need to focus on leveraging the **network programming** to develop your MCN's brand image.

The second type of content you should focus on creating is **Commissioned Programming**; this can be achieved by assisting your creators with obtaining brand sponsorships.

The brand sponsorship will pay for the cost involved in developing commissioned programming while also building relations with sponsors for developing **Original Programming** that features their products as paid product placements, which are necessary to mitigate the costs of developing Original Programming.

Advice for Making Your Original Programming Content

"~~Good~~, fast or cheap. Pick two."

"Good" is defined as productions above $1 million an episode as you would with a television show. This is much too costly for our medium.

"Fast & Cheap" is defined as Robert Rodriguez-style shooting;

- "*Creativity, not money, is used to solve problems.*"
- Strong emphasis on recycling existing assets or obtaining new assets that can be used multiple of ways.
- Barter or in-kind service exchanges to obtain out of budget necessities.

Again, I endorse a lean startup methodology for the growth of a business and apply these same sensibilities to the production of content.

The Legal Structure for Your MCN

I am not a lawyer and I cannot give you legal advice on how to structure your network as a legal entity. However, I will tell you how I setup my company and some of the things I considered when making the decisions on how I did so.

For networks, internal organization is key. This will be a company, and one with many pieces in the form of people with varying views and objectives. You should incorporate as a legitimate legal entity and not a sole proprietorship, which offers no benefits and puts substantial risk on yourself as an individual.

I first setup my company as an LLC and then switched to a C Corporation in Delaware when I looked to bring on investors. The benefits of Delaware incorporation are multi-folded; in addition to the franchise tax becoming dependent on the number of shares a company has issued, Delaware also has many years of corporate litigation history that has created a strong foundation of contract law in the States. The vast majority of angel investors and venture capitalists are familiar with Delaware C Corporations and consequently most tech companies are structured as such. More than 50% of Fortune 500 companies, and close to one million business entities, have made Delaware their home.

Nevada is the second most popular state to incorporate in given it has some similarities to Delaware given Nevada has made effort to design their courts, tax structures, and regulatory climates to cater to corporations in order to attract tax revenue for the state. I recommend you consult a seasoned business attorney who is familiar with Delaware and Nevada incorporation to assist you with deciding what is best for your YouTube network.

In addition to employees, you will end up with a large number of YouTube creators. Creators are rarely employees of the network; instead they are contractors who remain their own unique legal entities. Consequently, tax deductions related to employment are not removed from the payments given to a creator, as the network is simply collecting the channel revenue on behalf of the creator and taking a commission on the money in exchange for their services. This is why YouTube networks do not generally issue W-2s to creators and why this common criticism of networks is unwarranted; creators who think they deserve W-2s should re-examine their contract and see if they are considered an employee or a contractor, then consult with an accountant.

Some networks will begin with more resources than others, but no matter how they are started, the option to gain investors is always an advantage to moving forward and building the foundation for a business that can succeed.

While I would like to supply you with a template for a standard YouTube contract, unfortunately I am not a lawyer and I think it would be legally problematic for me to provide such a template in this book. What I suggest is that you collect several contracts from existing YouTube networks and analyse them with the assistance of an attorney experienced in entertainment deals for drafting your own creator contracts. This will also ensure you are educated on what kind of contract arrangement is standard to the industry.

The Organizational Structure of a Typical YouTube MCN Startup

In many ways a YouTube multi-channel network (MCN) startup is structured very similarly to a local television station. The core difference is that as YouTube is a search engine, there is a much greater reliance on having staff who specialize in online marketing than traditional kinds of promotion. The other difference is that as the bulk of a network's content is produced by freelance content contributors (the YouTube creators) the network has to employ talent management staff who provide a number of services for the creators.

In the following pages I'll briefly discuss the different departments within a typical MCN startup and what kind of work is done by the employees in each division.

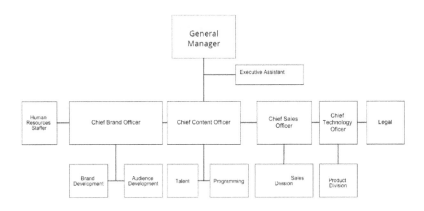

The General Manager

This is the individual responsible for overseeing the entire network operations the same way the general manager of a traditional television network would. The role might be called President or CEO, depending on the size of the MCN in question, but the duties of the role are always the same:

1. Executive the overall vision for the network, including talent management and platform development.

2.   Hire and manage employees of the division.

3.   Develop B2B relations and opportunities for the network.

The general manager needs to be quite knowledgeable about software development, the online video content business (especially its economics and practices).

The general manager must also possess a high degree of management skills. Some level of a micromanaging of the network divisions is necessary at the startup phase of the network in order to train staff to operate according to the culture you want your company to have, but the general manager needs to also know when it is time to allow the division leadership to run their ship without hand holding. You need a general manager who can be a focal point of decision-making at the launch of the network but can simultaneously train the early staff to become leaders of their divisions and replicate the decisions of the general manager without his / her personal involvement. Once your network grows to several hundred creators it is simply impractical for the general manager to be personally involved in every decision making process at the lower levels of the company, and the general manager must know when to let the lower tier employees do their thing and only intervene when there is a substantial problem the lower ends of the chain of command are unable to resolve.

Executive Assistant

Executive assistants handle executive/senior-level correspondence and phones; field viewer questions and complaints; manage the executive appointments calendar; process billing; in general, try to make the day go more smoothly for the General Manager.

Don't confuse the abundance of clerical duties with a lack of importance in this position. The executive assistant is often the person who determines who gains access to the General Manager, and thus this administrative position can be a powerful role at the network.

Chief Content Officer

Responsible for the production of all network 'Content'.

This is primarily....

1. Original programming
2. Commissioned programming
3. Website(s) content

The CCO works through Program Division Heads, who directly manage their departments.

The CCO also manages the Talent divisions via the Head of Talent, who ensures quarterly goals are reached. Because both Programming and Talent are managed by the CCO any coordination issues between the two departments can be quickly resolved by final decision of the CCO, who ensures they work together as right and left hands.

The CCO role can be performed by the General Manager until there are 4-5 Program Divisions, at which point it will require a dedicated individual in the position.

Programming

Programming Divisions are responsible for producing content in specific verticals (Games, Music, Food, etc.). This includes all content, from web series to blog articles.

Content produced by these divisions is used by the Audience Development Division for Scheduling.

As an example, the Games Program Division would...

- Operate the network Gaming news blog.
- Produce Original gaming shows.
- Work with gaming Talent to create Commissioned content.

Talent

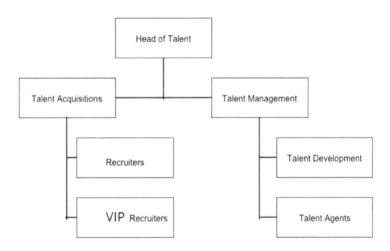

Talent Acquisitions is responsible for recruiting Talent (YouTube channels) for the different service tiers of the network.

- Recruiters focus on "rising Talent" who have between 5K - 500K views per month.

- VIP Recruiters focus on "VIP Talent" who have over 500K views per month.

Talent Management help guide Talent to career opportunities with the network.

- Talent Development runs workshops and training sessions for Talent personal development.
- Talent Agents work with the Program Divisions to match Talent to opportunities for Original or commission programming.

Chief Brand Officer

Manages the different brand promotional departments through two main divisions;

1. Brand Development
2. Audience Development

The multi-headed hydra that is "marketing" is broken up into smaller divisions specialized in their singular area.

To prevent confusion on who reports to whom, Audience Development will be responsible for Research, who will distribute their reports throughout the entire network to appropriate departments. This is also ideal as Research can be supervised by the same Audience Development head who supervises Customer Service and Scheduling; the two primary internal sources of audience data

Brand Division

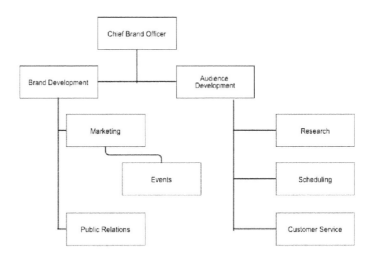

Brand Development

Brand Development is responsible for building brand awareness and communicating the network's value to the market.

Marketing is responsible for producing all advertising / promotional material and coordinating the Events (trade-shows, VidCon, workshops, etc.).

Public Relations manages the spread of information between the network and the public. PR handles all relationships with third-party media (blogs, journalists, TV shows, etc.).

Audience Development

Audience Development is responsible for satisfying and creating audience demand for the network's products.

Research analyzes audience metrics and identifies trends in the markets. This information is passed to Scheduling, Marketing and Program Divisions for original / commission content production.

Scheduling supervises the release of content on all mediums owned by the network (social media, websites, apps, mailing lists, etc.).

Customer Service handles all customer complaints about the network and its many divisions. Customer Service also handles Tech Support for the network apps and any network owned websites.

Sales Division

The Chief Sales Officer (CSO) is responsible for the hiring, training and management of the ad sales teams.

Ad Sales teams are broken into specific verticals: national, local and non-traditional.

National: Large brands on the Fortune 500 list.

Local: Small businesses which are local to a specific geographic region in which the content is relevant.

Non-traditional: Educational institutions, non-profits, political campaigns, etc.

All the ad sales products are identical (pre-rolls, product placement, branded show, etc.) but the teams focus exclusively on certain categories of customers, using sales staff who cater their pitches and sales styles to these specific classes of customers.

Technology Division

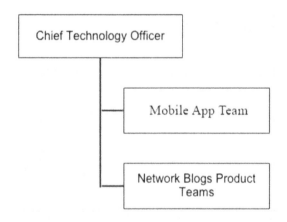

Responsible for supervising and ensuring the technology product milestones are achieved. Also hires the product development teams (web designers, programmers, GUI artists, database engineers, etc.).

The two main technology products are;

1. Network-owned website blogs
2. Network-owned mobile apps

You may not require a Technology division at the start but it is good to have considering proprietary technology is a key competitive advantage in the industry.

Legal Division

This division consists of your network's general counsel and a few paralegals to assist.

The main roles of Legal are:

1. Rights Clearances
2. Trademarking
3. Copyright Disputes (Content ID)
4. Contracts and Contract Dispute Arbitration

Human Resources

HR can be initially managed by a single individual who fields any employee complaints and works with department heads to address those complaints.

The HR staffer can also be assigned to identify individuals (both inside and outside) for roles within the company, and even conduct the initial interviews with the job applicants.

HR will also be responsible for recruiting interns from the local colleges.

As the network staff grows larger, additional assistants can be hired and the original HR staffer promoted to a HR manager position.

Four Keys to Success

In my experience there are four things that define a successful MCN startup and that you must include in your company when you build it.

1. Budget discipline & agile streamlined organization.

2. Strong work ethic expected of all employees and contractors.

3. Keen eye for matching rising talent with quality scripts.

4. Reward loyalty and good performance.

Choosing Your Niche

To identify the customer profile for your network you will need to be able to solve a problem. This is becoming ever more difficult as existing MCNs become more sophisticated and creators become better educated about what service is possible, but there are still ample opportunities if you are knowledgeable enough about the idiosyncrasies of the business.

For example, it is nigh-impossible to monetize a gaming focused channel on YouTube unless your channel is in an MCN. This is because YouTube's monetization employees tend to reject monetization of any video that contains gameplay footage in it, even if that video fully complies with YouTube's own policies for gameplay footage AND even if you have written permission from a developer. I am speaking from personal experience here; even if you produce gaming videos where the game's copyright owner has a public policy that allows anyone to monetize videos featuring gameplay (such as Minecraft and World of Warcraft) someone at YouTube is going to reject the monetization of your videos because for reasons I will never understand YouTube employs a lot of people in their monetization review department who do not care.

Now, an MCN is provided a special kind of account called a CMS, or Content Management Suite. As part of the agreement the MCN has with YouTube the MCN, not YouTube, is in charge of reviewing whether a video complies with YouTube's policies for monetization. This is important for gaming channels, because it means unless a copyright claim is made against the video the channel can monetize any video they submit for monetization. I can assure you the majority of MCNs interpret the monetization rules very loosely and go unpunished when they make violations.

The important thing is that due to the way YouTube poorly abides by its own policies YouTube itself forces all gaming channels to join an MCN in order to be able to monetize the videos. This is the primary reason I focused on gaming channels when I started Power Up TV.

You should also consider what services you can provide that have nothing to do with the CMS account itself; for example, you could provide creators who join your network with access to professional sound stages and equipment at no upfront cost. In the past I have found providing creators with access to a library of royalty free music loops to use as background music in their videos to be a popular incentive.

What Can You Do for Creators?

This is the most important question you can ask yourself. It is also the most important question that creators will ask when they consider joining your network.

I considered writing a book on salesmanship but the truth is there is already fantastic book on the subject that I could never hope to compete with; Selling the Wheel. If you are serious about starting a YouTube network in this highly competitive field, then you should read this book.

Generally, creators are looking for the followings things from an MCN:

1. Promotion: to help the creators build awareness of their content.
2. Brand deals: to help the creators earn money.
3. Production resources: such as cameras, lights, possibly even stage access and/or funding.
4. Community: a sense of belonging.

Your skill at advertising your ability to deliver these four things to creators will determine how successful your MCN is.

Why do YouTube Creators Join Networks?

It is crucial that you consider the benefits a creator obtains by signing a contract with a network. If you haven't put the thoughtful work into, you could be digging your own grave. It's not enough to just want to start a network; you have to offer something of perceived value.

Here are the most common reasons a creator chooses to join a network:

Help with Getting more Subscribers

Channel subscribers are a key metric in the YouTube community. If you get enough subscribers, YouTube will mail you a nice silver or gold plated YouTube play button to mount on your wall, which has similar status to possessing plated record album. Consequently, getting more subscribers is a key goal for many creators.

As a network you have the ability to build a large database of subscribers to all the channels who join your network. It is possible to consolidate the viewers across all channels in the network into a single email list that can be used to promote videos of other channel partners, thereby helping drive views -- and consequently new subscribers -- to any channels you like. This is a powerful incentive for creators to join your network, if you can deliver on the promise.

The most valuable benefit that YouTube creators will see in joining a network is the promise of promotion for their videos. This necessitates a high proficiency at promoting video content through a variety of channels, such as directly to viewers through mailing lists and social media profiles, while also convincing journalists to write promotional pieces about your creators and their work. It can be helpful to even create your own niche interest blogs where videos of your channel partners can be seeded to help build awareness.

Brand Expert Consulting

Networks are expected to hire a kind of talent manager who will work with its creators to assist them in planning out their long-term strategies for developing the channel into a profitable business. Most all creators who join a network expect to have a talent manager assigned to them, who will provide one-on-one coaching on the best ways to make money on the platform. If you can provide this incentive, you should do so.

However, keep in mind this information is being supplied for the interests of the network, too. This is also a consideration for the network itself. They have the flexibility and hopefully the funding to keep very qualified people working with them. With the advantage of multiple persons involved, you have access to better legal assistance as well.

Assistance with Content ID Disputes

There is a perception among creators that networks can assist when they get Content ID matches on their videos which the creator believes are unfair or unwarranted. This is true to an extent; there are many times a CMS holder places a match on a video that should not have had one, and the network staff can assist if they are skilled at reaching out to the legal departments of other media companies. However, it is usually more common for a creator to simply be misinformed on how copyright law works and the Content ID match was completely valid.

Regardless, if a popular creator has a lot of Content ID matches which are stopping them from monetizing their videos, they will often look for a network to join who can help them resolve the issues and recover the lost revenue.

Higher Potential Earnings

Many networks advertise that they offer higher ad rates than normal. This usually is a half-truth; very few networks have the ability to sell their own pre-roll ad inventory against videos in their networks, and those that do normally save this inventory for their most popular channels whom the advertisers want to target.

Whether in a network or not, the vast majority of a YouTube channel's ad inventory will be served by Google AdWords and the MCN has no part in these ad sales whatsoever.

Still, many creators will seek to join networks under the belief they will earn more money being with a network than without one. If you are able to deliver on this promise, you will be successful in the market.

Funding

Many networks promise to invest money into producing original content with the creators who join their networks, and this is often able to lure the more business minded creators into signing contracts with a network.

Having better access to working capital and can improve the quality of their content, the leverage of their brand, the market reach of advertising efforts, as opposed to dealing with the struggles of a single entrepreneur trying to find the production of a web series entirely by themselves.

Funding is nearly always reserved for channel creators which have already proven successful in the market and earned many hundreds of thousands of subscribers, but this fact does not deter many creators from joining networks who are just starting out and erroneously think the network will give them large bags of money for their pet project.

Common Reasons Why Creators Don't Join Networks

Just as there are reasons why creators join networks, there are also reasons why creators don't --or at least, why they are reluctant to do so. These are the most common.

Vague Terms in the Contract or Misconceptions about Joining

The chance to work with a YouTube multi-channel network can be extremely advantageous to YouTube creators. Many can easily benefit from resources a network can provide such as additional funding, more exposure, and better strategies.

On the other hand, for some creators joining a network can be considered a bad choice. There are many creators who have suffered at the hands of their networks, entering into very one-sided agreements that do not benefit the creator at all. This has resulted in a very vocal portion of the YouTube creator community to have lost enthusiasm for running their channels, and in the worst cases even a large percentage of their own businesses. Unexpectedly many creators have found themselves involved in toxics relationships with their networks and you can read about many horror stories related to these incidents with a simple search engine query.

Many networks write up very complicated contracts that express terms in vague ways. These contracts are sometimes written by very experienced lawyers who are skilled at using legalese to trick the layperson into entering a deal that is very unfavourable to them. On the other side of the fence you have some networks who hire lawyers that are very inexperienced with the entertainment industry who draft contracts that are hard to understand for those creators that are knowledgeable about what is the norm within the industry.

It can backfire on a network to attempt manipulating a producer with false promises or other immoral practices. You will want you lawyers to be as transparent as possible when drafting the contracts for creators to join the network.

Fear of losing control of their rights

Ownership of the YouTube channel owner's content is a large factor. Each network differs regarding their contractual agreements and what rights the creator will retain as far as original rights to the content they create. Most networks only ask for the right to use the material in promotion while the creator is with the network, but some networks attempt to slip in language that gives the network the right to make merchandise featuring the creators and not share this revenue with them.

While it is true as a network you need to maximize the revenue opportunities to help the network grow, on the other hand, a network with no partners associated with it will have no content to air. It is unrealistic to expect creators to give up a significant portion of their intellectual property rights just to join a network. There has to be an equal exchange; such as the creators producing the content, but your network is going to fund its production. The relationship has to be mutually beneficial.

If you want to gain perpetual rights to creators' content even though you are doing nothing to help them make that content, then you may want to consider starting a different business than a YouTube network because it's very unlikely to work out for you.

AdSense Ownership
The fear of losing control of an AdSense account is one of the most common myths associated with YouTube networks. It is largely due to many creators misunderstanding the relationship between a YouTube CMS account and their personal channel.

When creating and managing a YouTube channel as an individual, you must connect that channel to an AdSense account associated with the Google account. However, for a network, we use an account called a Content Management Suite (CMS) which can associate multiple channels with a single AdSense account. As a result, a YouTube network never has the ability to login to a creator's personal AdSense account unless the creator specifically gives the account username and password to that account.

Once again for clarity, when a YouTube channel joins a network, all advertising revenue earned by the channel goes into the AdSense account of the network owner. It never goes into the AdSense account of the channel creator. Networks have no ability to access a creator's AdSense account unless the network has the login information for the AdSense account in question.

Less Control Over Content

Creators are, well, creative types. Having less control over the type of content you produce and how you artistically express it is a huge factor for writers, painters, musicians and even YouTube filmmakers. There's no getting over this for anyone accustomed to self-expression. The irony is that successful creators want to produce on the merits of sharing a unique message all their own.

If a creator feels their artistic license will be taken away when joining a network, then the creator will feel they will be losing the very thing that made the creator so successful in the first place. The conflict will be an ongoing one with different interests involved. A network's main objective may be to earn money, but most artists are simply looking to make a healthy pay check while they make more art.

Frustration at the Reality of How YouTube Monetization Works

There is no way for a network to only monetize specific videos, such as those created after the creator joined the network or those videos which the network helped produce. Monetization for channels is all or nothing; all revenue earned by the channel will go into the network CMS account.

This concern probably gets under the skin of all creators, especially the most popular ones. They invested years of their life building a brand, and now they have to give a substantial amount of their revenue on years of back library to a network just to join it for assistance with making new videos.

For all successful YouTube creators, there are likely years of sweat and tears that simply don't get accounted for when they sign with a network who will benefit monetarily from the years of work they did in the past.

This concern will be the largest obstacle to overcome with popular creators. To get a valuable channel to join your network you will need to offer a service that justifies earning a percentage of revenue from the past library of the creator. If you have a reasonable response to this question, then you will be successful at convincing popular creators to sign up to your network.

Again, the relationship between a network and creators must be viewed as mutually beneficial. If it's not, the creators won't join.

Generating Leads

Lead generation is one of the most critical tasks for any business, and a YouTube MCN is no exception. YouTube MCNs actually tend to experience a high amount of churn, so you need a constant flow of new channels signing up to keep growing.

For generating leads I developed proprietary software (i.e. scrape bots) to data-mine YouTube to harvest emails from channels that met the criteria that fit my customer profiles -- those creators I wanted to join the network. I also ran data-mining software on various Facebook Groups that were focused on YouTube video creation. I also ran meetup groups, such as the one in Austin and the one I started in Long Beach, specifically to create a community of YouTubers to help build awareness of my networks. All of these things helped me grow a large list of potential creators to market to.

Using the methods I described it is possible to build a lead sheet and acquire customers even if you never knew any YouTubers before. Honestly, these two methods -- scrapping information from Facebook Groups, and starting communities using Meetup.com -- these are two methods everyone should use to grow a customer base for any startup; it is not something specific to operating a YouTube network.

Meetup events are held at your headquarters to both generate leads and build a tribe around your brand.

Website SEO is also important, and it's one of the areas most MCNs are very bad at. I was able to successfully rank Power Up TV on the first page of results for search phrases like, "YouTube gaming partnership" specifically because most gaming MCNs like Machinima rely more on word of mouth and press to recruit leads, and do not utilize a very good SEO strategy. I would say the bulk of Power up TV's leads were generated due to high first page rankings of the site for keyword phrases related to YouTube networks.

How to Get a YouTube CMS Account

Obtaining a YouTube CMS account with the channel rollup tool enabled is one of the most notoriously difficult things you will ever try to do in a business. YouTube's requirements for obtaining one vary depending on who you are and who you know. I know of one MCN who was able to obtain a CMS without any hassles whatsoever simply because the founder was related to the prominent founder of another MCN and so he was able to leverage connections with YouTube's upper-management. By contrast I've had to meet very intense requirements, such as hundreds of millions of hours of video watch time, to obtain a CMS account.

So here's the reality; unless you have 100s of millions of hours of watch time on your channel in the past 90 days OR you are best buds with someone influential within YouTube, you are very unlikely to get a CMS account and sign an MCN agreement with YouTube. In recent years the company has really circled the wagons around the program and made it very difficult for new players to enter the market. There are many reasons for this, ranging from favouritism of YouTube employees toward certain MCNs to YouTube upper management simply not wanting to invest new resources into supporting MCNs. Knowledge of this will not assist you in securing a CMS account.

If you need advice on how grow a channel to have millions of views, I suggest you purchase my book *The Lean Channel: YouTube for Entrepreneurs* (http://amzn.to/1VkOvSD). Everything you need to know to grow a big channel is in this book.

On the other hand, if you DO have the necessary watch time and YouTube still isn't giving you the time of day, the problem could be no one at YouTube has ever heard of your company before. When I have had this problem in the past I addressed it by conducting targeted ad campaigns on LinkedIn and Facebook that would only be seen by people who worked at YouTube's San Bruno and Los Angeles offices. The promoted links pointed to articles and videos which talked about the success the company was having at various things. I created this campaign myself and designed it to build awareness of the company within the community of YouTube employees. After a month of this, we finally started getting some cooperation from YouTube.

Another route to go is to simply enter into an agreement with an established MCN to purchase a CMS account from them, which has the channel rollup tool unlocked. This is how a few MCNs have entered the market. The details on each deal vary greatly, so unfortunately I cannot give you any kind of guide on how to structure such a deal. You're simply going to have to reach out to various MCNs (especially the foreign MCNs based in countries like India) and see what you can do with them.

Your YouTube Network Dashboard

If by some chance you manage to get a CMS account and sign the MCN agreement, your first order of business will be to create a Partner dashboard. This is a third party application (always cloud-based) that uses the YouTube API to help manage your channels.

Perhaps the most important role of the dashboard is that it must enable payments to be made, tracked and sent out for the network's partners. A YouTube CMS account, while filled with many useful functions, is terribly non-user friendly and does not allow you to do very basic things like identify how much revenue each channel has earned and pay them a % of it. The downloadable monthly reports will tell you how much money individual videos in the entire network earned, but will not tell you which channels the video belongs to.

This means you need to develop a tool that can decipher the downloadable report and match the videos to their respective channels, and then perform the calculations necessary to determine how much money you should pay that channel based on your ad revenue channel agreements with the channel owner.

Your network also needs a viable way of tracking individual channel viewer analytics well as channel earnings. This means the dashboard needs to interpret the data it pulls from YouTube's API to create a reporting system that automatizes much of the cross-referencing of useful stats.

The Partner dashboard also needs to serve other functions, such as allowing you to communicate with the partners for tech support or allow them access to the special benefits of membership (such as downloadable templates, royalty free music, etc.).

Many Partner Dashboards these days are fully integrated into the MCN application process, meaning the dashboard itself serves as the system for approving and rejecting channels to join your network.

Option A) Developing your own Dashboard

Depending on how you do the software development and what kinds of features you want, it will cost between $15,000 to $180,000 to develop a proprietary Partner dashboard system. The costs depend on such factors as how many features you want it to have and if you use near-shore developers or those based in the United States.

I have supervised the development of a system which cost $25,000 and included features for earnings tracking and payment, along with the ability to approve or reject channels. It also had features for allowing channel partners to recruit other channels and earn a % of revenue from the network's share (essentially, a recruit-a-friend referral offer). Lastly it also allowed for the creation of subnetworks.

To create a dashboard, you will need to be a good product manager.

Option B) Choosing not to develop a proprietary dashboard

If developing your own Partner dashboard seems above your paygrade you can license pre-existing systems from other MCNs such as Bent Pixels. This has the advantage of giving you what you want quickly, but has the disadvantage of costing about the same as to develop your own without the ability to customize it for your specific needs.

Your best bet to start a new network is as a subnetwork to another MCN. In exchange for giving you the ability to add channels to a CMS which that parent MCN controls, the parent MCN will generally take 50% of your cut of the ad revenue you'd be collecting from a channel. On the bright side you will use the third party dashboard system the parent MCN has created to manage your channel, which will save you the money and time of developing your own. On the downside you are completely at the mercy of the parent MCN to pay you correctly.

There are several MCNs which take on subnetworks -- Freedom, Bent Pixels and BroadbandTV are the primary three -- but to be honest, I cannot honestly recommend any of them. I started Power Up TV under Freedom and the experience was not very ideal, for reasons I unfortunately cannot go into in this book. But depending on your goals, starting out as a subnetwork might be good way to get the ball rolling. It was the case for Power Up TV.

That said, when choosing the subnetwork route you are certain to encounter difficulties dealing with these middle men and it is something you will need to decide on your own if you want to do.

Obtaining YouTube Certification

To be a recognized YouTube multi-channel network you must become a YouTube Certified company. To obtain "YouTube Certified" status your company must establish that the lesser of 3 or 25% of its full-time employees as personally certified pursuant to the YouTube Certification Program.

In order to get an employee eligible to take the exam, you must have their email address associated with your YouTube CMS account as a CMS manager. This is currently accomplished by connecting the Google plus account of your employee to your CMS account, but as YouTube is always making changes it may be different by the time you read this.

Having valid YouTube Company Certification status entitles your company to:

1. Be listed on YouTube's publicly accessible Certified Companies page that contains information about your company.

2. Advertise the fact that Company is "YouTube Certified" in the specific area(s) in which it has qualified;

3. Use the YouTube Certified logo graphic on your website and marketing materials.

Shortly after obtaining a YouTube CMS account with channel-roll up enabled, YouTube will ask you to select employees to take the exam. You will have a brief period of time to have your employees certified. It may be easier to simply hire employees who already possess the certification status.

Understanding Content ID and its Purpose for MCNs

While a comprehensive guide to using Content ID falls well outside the purpose of this book, Content ID is such a crucial feature of YouTube networks that I would be negligent to not provide at least some information. Even inside large, well established networks Content ID is one of the most misused tools and to avoid mistakes I think it is important that I talk about what it is, what it is for, and how not to screw up when you use it.

The business of a YouTube network is in video content. The content itself is a product. Thus it should be no surprise that content owners wish to protect this asset from copyright infringers who re-upload videos without authorization.

Infringing on the intellectual property of others is a huge offense, and the work of others should be protected as a result. The laws are stringent and the costs are very high for infringement. The copyrights of artists have historically been protected and the majority of victims of copyright infringement will have the backing of the courts.

Yet lawsuits are very costly matters. Our legal system was simply not setup to deal with every thirteen-year-old with a laptop re-uploading their favourite music videos to their personal YouTube channels. It is not cost effective for rights holders to sue millions of people around the world, and yet they need a level of protection to ensure they can monetize the work they own.

The Content ID toolset came about in 2006 as a result of the lawsuits filed against YouTube early in its lifespan by major content owners. As the host of the content, YouTube is legally required to submit to DMCA takedown notifications yet trying to address every claim on millions of videos would quickly exhaust YouTube's staff in a never-ending pile of takedown requests to examine. The solution was for YouTube to develop a fingerprinting algorithm which could identify the audio and video assets which have been uploaded to YouTube by users who do not have sufficient rights.

Yet, Content ID is simply not about removing videos from YouTube; it can also permit users to upload videos to their channels and still allow the rights holder to monetize the videos with ads. This is the most common use of Content ID. In most cases it is better to simply monetize the videos rather than remove them.

How Does Content ID Work?

Content ID is very much what it sounds like. It identifies video content that is unique from other video content in the same manner that our fingerprints are unique and can be used to identify us. This digital identity is stored in an asset list uploaded to the CMS account and collected as different information from the actual video itself. All content has a unique voice, message and configuration that makes it clearly distinctive and different from others. This is true even for content produced in the same genre.

How is this possible? The uniqueness of a video asset can be analysed through visual patterns on monitor displays and through the frequencies emitted by the video's audio output. Because of this, a YouTube user won't be able to trick the platform by uploading the same video using a different name. Content ID analyses the content of a video, not its field meta-data.

All content uploaded to the YouTube hosting platform can be analysed by the Content ID system based on how close the video's asset ID —consisting of visual patterns and audio patterns—matches an already existing video file on the site held in an asset list by a CMS account holder.

If Content ID locates a video that matches an asset in the CMS holders list, both parties involved will be notified. The user who YouTube recognizes as the original owner of the content will be given a few options, such as to monitor the analytics of the unauthorized videos, or to remove it completely from the website and issue a copyright strike to the uploader. The CMS account holder can also monetize the video and earn from the infringer's effort.

As for the person who's been recognized by the system as the infringer, they will also be given the option to challenge the notification of infringement by filing a counter DMCA notification, but this can work against them if the account holder decides to persist in the claim. Nevertheless, not all cases where someone is accused of copyright infringement are entirely accurate. In fact, it is possible for Content ID to match a video which the CMS owner does not exclusively own, due to failures of the CMS owner to follow the rules for creating matches.

For example, sometimes a network will add the episodes of a gaming channel to Content ID, even though much of the video consists of content that features gameplay and audio recorded from the videogame featured in the video. This will cause Content ID to match all kinds of videos that feature that same audio and video clip. What the content owner should have done is make a video that had only the original footage and audio in it, without any of the clips featuring the video game in question. This would create a valid match data set, and focus only on unauthorized re-uploads of the original content.

As YouTube's specific methods of using and appealing Content ID matches changes every few months (YouTube likes to update their software often) I won't provide any detailed instructions on how to do matches. If you obtain access to Content ID then your partner representative will provide you with a guide for how to use the system.

How Do Networks Use Content ID?

YouTube networks primarily use Content ID to protect the rights of their clients. Many prominent YouTube creators have their videos re-uploaded by other users; sometimes, armies of them. There is an underground market of black hat marketers who re-upload popular videos to YouTube with affiliate links in the video description in order to game the search algorithms to make money. These are not just a handful of channels; it's the systematic creation of thousands of channels by a single blackhat marketer.

Generally speaking, a single channel owner cannot get Content ID for themselves. To qualify for the tool, you usually need to have a large amount of watch time (hundreds of thousands of hours watched) and to have a lot of unauthorized uploading of your videos occurring. This means a popular channel with hundreds of thousands of subscribers often does not qualify for Content ID on their own. Because the primary source of many YouTube creators' revenue is ads, this re-uploading of their videos cuts deeply into their earnings. Consequently, many large channels join YouTube networks specifically to get the protection of Content ID for their videos and recover lost revenue.

There are many arguments people make for why Content ID should be available to everyone, and while I can agree to an extent that YouTube often makes it more difficult to obtain the tool than necessary, I also know how abusive Content ID can be in the wrong hands. It is very difficult to monetize public domain work on YouTube because many Content ID owners will ignore the rules and add public domain content to their asset lists. This allows them to monetize all uploads of public domain movies, cartoons and even music. Yes, it's nearly impossible for a pianist to upload their own recording of anything from Beethoven or Mozart because they will be slammed with Content ID matches from a multiple networks all claiming exclusive rights in different territories. The lack of YouTube concern for regulating the abuses of Content ID by large networks is perhaps my single biggest criticism of YouTube as a company.

Superman The Mad Scientist 1941

A Content ID match against a public domain work claimed by WaterTower, a subsidiary of Warner Brothers.

As an example of a Content ID abuse; the Fleischer Studios cartoons of Superman (including the music created specifically for these cartoons) have been in the public domain for many decades due to the failure of National Telefilm Associates to renew their copyright in the 1960s, making any legal claim of distribution rights not legally enforceable.

Yet YouTube will consistently support certain Content ID owners in their claim to own the content, regardless of the DMCA rules. The only way for uploaders to use the material would be to file a lawsuit, which is simply impractical for the vast majority of YouTube users.

The Content ID system therefore creates a method for wealthy and well connected companies to YouTube to monetize whatever videos they want, even if they do not possess exclusive rights to the content. As a network owner this may appeal to you, but as a startup you will find it frustrating as public domain content has historically served to help new television stations supplement their libraries. The inability for new channels to leverage public domain content due to Content ID abuses is a barrier to entry and another way that established media conglomerates discourage competition.

Anyway, having said all of this, I do believe the Content ID tool is necessary. There is no other way for a network to protect the intellectual rights of creators, therefore, the use of Content ID is necessary. I simply encourage you to use the tool in a responsible fashion.

As a network owner charged with using Content ID you would be best served with following the best known practices with integrity and honesty. Doing so only ensures that your company will build a solid reputation in the market as a brand that can be trusted by both creators and viewers. Also keep in mind the YouTube Content tool is a privilege that can be taken away quickly, which will hurt both your bottom line and reputation. If you cut yourself off from this earning potential by greedily abusing the tool, it may then become impossible to return to using it in the future.

This is a good time to remind network owners that any falsification on the YouTube platform will lead to restricted access and even complete deactivation of an account. This is something you should avoid at all costs, so keep your content in good standing. The best rule of thumb is to take infringement of another's original content very seriously by never creating matches for content that is not wholly exclusively owned by the creator, and ensuring your creators do not infringe on other users' rights, either.

Dealing with Creators

As a YouTube network your primary customer is the talent -- the YouTube creators which you represent. So I felt I should give some general advice on how to interact with them.

Many creative types will not listen to anything that resembles a business focused conversation. They just want to play with their webcams all day, and push content into the ether that is YouTube Search without any rational strategy for how their videos will get discovered.

Additionally, creators are a naturally suspicious lot who almost universally dislike MCNs. This is largely because MCNs tend to break their promises to creators, but it is also because creators are often reluctantly forced into joining an MCN in order to be able to monetize their channels, giving up anywhere from 10% to 60% of their ad revenue just for the privilege of being able to monetize videos they should have been able to monetize to start with. The simple reality is certain video categories such as gaming are difficult to monetize outside of a YouTube network, as YouTube's monetization team often rejecting these videos for monetization even if they comply with the Terms of Service rules for fair use.

A lot of creators feel they shouldn't be required to give away a percentage of their earnings just to monetize videos they should legally be able to monetize, and this is a sentiment I cannot completely disagree with.

Thus, it is not entirely incorrect for creators to view MCNs as a kind of racket they are forced to participate in because of the way YouTube handles monetization request reviews. Unfortunately, because there are few alternative ways to monetize online videos at the indie level outside of YouTube's platform, creators are forced to play by the rules which YouTube and the MCNs have constructed in their favour.

As a new player to the market who has yet to screw over any creators, you have the opportunity to shape a brand message about being honest and transparent -- and provide real value to those creators that join your MCN.

The easiest way to deal with creators is to be honest and upfront with them at all times. If you cannot deliver on something, then don't promise it. When they are disgruntled, take the time to talk to them about it and come to a resolution that works for both sides.

Generally, creators believe more in receiving than in giving; for examples, they are not at all interested in assisting you with lead generation, marketing of your network or even writing positive reviews of your service unless they are compensated for these actions. This is not entirely unexpected because creators are their own legal entities and unless you've built in a reward mechanic, they gain no advantage to the network growing larger. This is why I recommend you build a good affiliate system for your dashboard that will compensate creators for recruiting their friends into the network.

As far as coordinating cross-promotion between channels -- which a creator ought to view as beneficial to themselves -- it is also tough to get creators to collaborate with one another. In my experience even if a creator agrees to do so, they very often fail to deliver on their side of the arrangement once one party has gotten what they wanted. I've talked before about creators not being very trusting of networks but this door also swings both ways; I've probably met more creators who cannot be trusted to keep their word based on handshake deals.

This is something you should always keep in mind with creators. Even though you should help them as much as you can, you also need to think in the best interest of the MCN itself. If creators promise to do something in exchange for something you are doing for them, this agreement should be enshrined in a contract to ensure both parties do what they say they will do, and that there will be consequences for either partying failing to do their share. This is a fair and proper business dealing.

If a creator will not sign a contract for a service which requires them to do something themselves, you should assume the creator does not want to do that service. This can be due to many different reasons -- sometimes to do with restrictions on other contract agreements they have made with other parties which prohibits them from agreeing to the terms -- but it can also just be based on the creator's ego and laziness. Sorting out which it is, must be done on a case by case basis.

The other thing you should consider is YouTube creators at all subscriber levels will often align themselves with a talent manager. These individuals are very rarely a legitimate talent agent who is licensed by the state of California and consequently their level of skill at managing the careers of the creators they represent can be as different as night and day. I will say that I have met more worthless amateur "managers" who wouldn't be able to recognize a bad deal if it kicked them in the head, than I have good ones who genuinely assist their clients. This can often play into the network's hands, but a talent manager who really hasn't got a clue can also intentionally sabotage your recruiting efforts because they are afraid of losing their client once the creator starts getting quality advice from the network staff. I can't really give you any good advice on how to deal with talent managers that represent creators because the frank reality is many creators are so misinformed by their peers on how the entertainment industry works, it is virtually impossible to convince them the way they think about things is incorrect.

You should focus your resources on casting a wide recruitment net and build value to the level a creator will weigh their imagined cons against the very real pros of joining your network, and the genuine value your company offers will defeat their imaginary fears. Don't invest too heavily on trying to recruit a specific creator who is on the fence, because there are many other creators who know a good deal when they see one. There are over a billion YouTube channels out there; don't become obsessed with just a handful of them.

Lastly I suggest you do not simply have creators directly emailing your employee's personal work inboxes for support, as this makes it difficult for your staff to manage the requests for support.

You should set up a CRM like ZenDesk or FreshDesk to handle customer support tickets, and this will actually make it easier for you to track the analytics related to the health of your network -- you can see if your employees are responding quickly and properly to address talent needs by reviewing the dashboard analytics of the CRM. Simply having the ability to issue a survey after every support ticket is closed will lead to your community managers working harder to help the creators, as they are aware they will be reviewed on their performance.

Dealing with YouTube Employees

There is no point in hiding this; YouTube is a very difficult company to deal with. The employees generally are not passionate about the online video space and actively look for excuses to not help creators address problems. It is my personal belief that one of the reasons YouTube likes MCNs is because they reduce YouTube's need to provide customer service for the majority of its creator community. The MCNs instead provide this support to address the most common questions, and the MCNs only turn to YouTube partner support when there are bugs to report.

This is just my opinion as an observer having worked with YouTube staff from the outside, but in many ways the corporate culture at YouTube seems designed to ensure that employees are terrified of their bosses and thus are unwilling to make introductions for people outside the company.

I have this belief because on more than one occasion I have had a mid-level YouTube employee express fear at the prospect of making an introduction to their boss, as for some reason managers at YouTube like to think themselves beyond approach. Worse, while you might think employees at YouTube would know who to direct you to if you have a question they cannot answer, I'm continually baffled at how factionalized YouTube as a company is; the people in one department don't seem to interact much with anyone outside that department.

This is so bad that YouTube Space LA employees have almost zero interaction with anyone who works in the San Bruno headquarters.

This fractioning and lack of communication between departments also creates problems in the administration of YouTube services to the public: for example, there are multiple training programs for creators ran by YouTube (for example, the Certification programs, the YouTube Space programs and the Creator Bootcamp programs), and none of them have anything to do with each other, even though they cover pretty much the same subject matter. They are all ran by different departments, too.

My last piece of advice on interacting with YouTube is the most important: In order to deal with YouTube successfully you need to have a YouTube employee champion you from the inside. This champion must hold a sufficiently senior position within the company that gives the champion decision making power. Anyone with a position lower than a Department Head will be utterly useless at assisting you with solving problems.

Dealing with Advertisers and Sponsors

You should familiarize yourself with my book *YouTube Sponsorships: How Creators Like You Can Fund Your Channel* (*http://amzn.to/1QQtPyX*). This will provide you a lot of information about how to go about developing pitches and such, and in this chapter I won't be going over any of the material I discussed in that book.

In general advertisers and sponsors are the easiest people for a network to deal with. Marketers have no qualms with spending money for campaigns, because that is what their job is about. Primarily what they want to see is a clear indication that you can deliver on the promises your pitch makes. So long as you can do this, you won't have too much difficulty winning over the decision makers and their underlings. The trouble comes when you have very little to present and offer to the brands, and that is where only the most daring of salesmanship can assist.

Speaking of trouble, your largest problem will be that many of the YouTubers who join your network simply do not have the necessary criteria that brands are looking for when looking for talent endorsements.

This can be due to many factors, but it's usually because the quality of their videos is low, and the advertisers only want to pay for a quality representation of their brand.

The second problem is sites like Famebit have created a large community of YouTubers who think their endorsement is worth the cost of the product and what it costs to ship it to the creator to make a video endorsement. These YouTubers don't actually earn money -- or if they do, it's something miniscule like $100. I don't know about you, but it takes me the better part of a day to plan, shoot, edit, upload and SEO even a 5-minute video of myself talking to the camera. Only earning $100 for a day of work is not the most efficient usage of my time.

Unfortunately, most YouTubers don't value their time correctly. Worse, they treat their channel like a hobby and are delighted that someone wants to "sponsor" them. It's more ego than business for these YouTubers, and sadly there is a lot of them out there over-saturating the market for popular niches like gaming and beauty. The brands are becoming more and more aware of this, which makes it harder to get even five figure deals for your talent.

So, what do you do then? The trick is to find a creator who produces good quality content AND specializes in an audience demographic that is normally difficult for advertisers to reach, and sell brands on the value of your talent as their representative to these hard to reach consumers. Recruit that creator and train them on how to re-think about their personal brand and the value of their time.

An easy way to do this is to simply say to a creator, "You're undervaluing yourself and your brand. You can get more money and I can help you".

Of course, you then must filter out the creators who think they aren't worth more, those who want to argue about artistic expressions and creative control, and other such trivial things. I know a lot of creators think they know it all, but they don't know what they don't know. And many of them don't know brands spend millions of dollars advertising their products and are willing to pay six figures or more for the right brand representative to step forward and plug their products to a mass number of people.

Furthermore, in my opinion, any talent who argue about creative control over an advertisement for someone else's product does not have a professional attitude and you should not invest much time trying to convince them to become more successful. You won't be able to reach them until they wake up one day with an epiphany about how many opportunities they are missing.

Let's talk about some popular categories for endorsements, if only so I can explain to you the issues facing you when you select certain niches.

Beauty is a good category because the products are made cheaply but sold for a high mark-up, but the main problem you have is all the female vloggers who are content just to get free lipstick and crap. So you have to find a niche within the beauty category; if you want to make real money with this creator through endorsements, it can't just be a creator who does generic makeup tips. There's like a million of those channels out there.

For beauty, a micro niche would be, as an example, something minority focused, like goths or hair extensions for African-American females. Something that is specific and subcultural, aimed at people who will spend an over-usual amount of money on specialty beauty products.

The thing to focus on is that companies who manufacture niche products for a niche market will pay for quality exposure to that niche market. Even if they normally give products away to vloggers, if you can promise them a high % of a certain demographic will see the video and that the video will be a quality representation of their brand, they will pay for that guaranteed exposure.

That said, once you make that promise to the advertisers you then have to prove the numbers; you must provide some proof the demographics are who you say they are. The easiest way to do this is for the talent to conduct an email survey of their followers.

"What? An email list?", you might say.

Yes, I know. Most YouTube creators don't even have an email list. I know, I've been pitched by enough big YouTubers (millions of subscribers here) to know many of these creators just stumble into their fame and have no idea about the most basic of basic marketing methods, of which email list generation most certainly is.

However, this gives you the opportunity to demonstrate your expertise as the business pro that you are. Once you get a creator to sign up, you will coordinate with the creator to produce a giveaway that will require the creator's followers to supply you with an email address in order to enter. The giveaway doesn't even have to be amazing; it can be something trivial and silly, like a USB memory card or an autographed headshot. A personal 10 minute Skype session. It just needs to be something the talent's fans will care about and that won't cost you more than $100 total.

So, no, you do not need to giveaway a chance to win a million dollars and make things complicated. I've done the latter and I'm here to tell you; the engagement is the same as with a chance to win something that is worth $100 or less.

Perhaps you are not an email list building expert. Maybe you don't know jack about email list building. That's okay, fortunately for you, I do and it's easy peasy. Since you bought my book I will talk you through the process of setting up a fail-proof giveaway so you can get 60% or more of your talent's fans to gladly hand you their email address.

Step 1. Build a Wordpress site for the talent (if they don't already have one).

So basically my first step is to build a website with the ability to come up with an email list. The website doesn't have to be complex at all. It doesn't even have to show the talent's videos. It just needs to have the very basic branding of the talent on it, a photo or two, and some text. Maybe a single blog post. It really doesn't matter because the only thing the fans will care about right now is entering the giveaway.

Step 2. Buy a Wordpress plugin

In particular, you need two plugins.

Optin-Panda
* http://codecanyon.net/item/optin-panda-for-wordpress/10224279

Social Locker.
* http://codecanyon.net/item/social-locker-for-wordpress/3667715

First install Social Locker, then Opt-in Panda. The latter is an extension for the former.

Also, I like to use what is called a "welcome mat on" my blogs, which is a free install from SumoMe. It makes it so every time someone comes to my blog, they are asked to join my mailing list (although they can still click down to just read the blog).

Here's an example of what that looks like,

Now there are some people out there -- I call them "whiner babies" -- who think this kind of tactic turns certain people off from your blog. And maybe it does, but you don't care about those whiner babies because they don't help you make any money. Screw them!

Who you should care about are the people who look at this welcome mat and say, "*Yeah, I want more information from you,*" and sign up to your mailing list.

For me, that's around 1,000 new people a month who opt into my list because they want to learn more from me.

Just letting you know.

Again, there are YouTube creators out there who think they know what they do not know. Sadly, even successful YouTubers generally owe their success to someone else embedding their videos on a website with a huge following, or the YouTube algorithms just promoting the heck out of them when Lady Luck shines her light upon them.
Don't assume popular YouTube creators understand the finer points of digital marketing. I've met very few creators who actually do, and I've met a lot of them.

Email list building is key. Do it right and you will fly even if Lady Luck hates your guts, because you've taken your destiny out of her hands.

Screw Lady Luck, Tell Me More About Using an Email List to Make Money

While there is much you can do with an email list, for the purpose of convincing advertisers, you want to survey the list and get people to fill out their information about gender, age and location via mailing address.

People are often reluctant to give this information over the internet, so stress how it is necessary to be entered for the fan to be shipped contest items, should they win the giveaway.

You can also ask the fans key things like what their preferred products are related to that industry, which is fine even if they don't mention the specific company you want to solicit. All companies have a customer profile they are targeting, and this profile target is people who are fans of that brand's competitors. The goal of marketing campaigns is rarely to convince consumers to use a brand new product, but rather to switch from using the competitor's product and instead purchase the advertiser's product. So ask those signing up for the giveaway questions about their favourite brands, and use that information when pitching their competitors!

Email lists are powerful for more than just information, too. They can also be used to build a digital marketing campaign to promote the video you produce for the brand client. You can literally import your email list into Facebook Power Editor and conduct targeted video ad campaigns at the people whose email address can be matched to a Facebook account -- which in my experience is pretty much all of them.

(Most people only have 1 email address they use for everything. People like me with hundreds of email addresses I manage in spreadsheets are rare.)

So, with an email list new options open up to you which can make you more competitive in a brand deal. You can not only know who your audience demographic is for a channel and use that fo information when selling a video endorsement of a product, but you can also tell the advertiser for an additional cost you can do a targeted Facebook ad campaign to your followers to ensure they see the video and/or any other ad that brand wants you to promote to this difficult to reach audience!

Furthermore, you can use your own email list to create a customer profile you can use for paid ad campaigns to grow the audience for your talent, or help a brand better refine their own customer profile by supplying detailed info about their desired customer they may not already have.

Using the Facebook Audience Insights tool, you can apply filters to target only people who are certain ages, genders, geographic location, married, single, certain income levels, like certain companies or brands, and find commonalities.

To further add, once you isolate this segment to target you can build a "look-alike" audience where Facebook will add other user accounts to your ad campaign that are not in your original email list, but whose interests, age, gender, sex, etc. are all identical to the people in your email list, greatly expanding the reach of the ad while maintaining the integrity of the customer profile you have generated using the mailing list.

How to Locate the Right Brands for your Talent

This requires the most leg work.

My advice is to look at who is making offers on micro-campaign websites like Famebit that have customers which probably fit the demographic of the talent you are working with. Track down their websites and contact their marketing people. You can also use LinkedIn to find the marketing people at certain companies.

You can also look at lists of booth holders at conventions like VidCon and Playlist Live, or other conventions within the specialty niche of your talent. Often, all of these conventions have a bunch of exhibitors trying to get YouTubers to endorse products and that they have a budget for attending conventions even once shows they have a decent sized marketing budget.

Remember, it's easier to get a brand that is already trying to get YouTubers to do video endorsements of a product, than to convince a brand that doesn't do it to begin doing so. Take the path of least resistance whenever possible.

If nothing else, you can always reach out to creative agencies that represent brands and convince them to include your talent in the campaigns they are already doing for those brands. Then what you and the talent get paid is just a slice of a much larger budget that is already being spent.

Hell, building a relationship with a creative agency that already has an approved budget for spending on endorsements will probably get you paid faster, too.

Dealing with the Press

In general, the press has no idea what is happening in the online video space, and even less of an idea in the YouTube MCN niche. This is especially true of traditional entertainment press journalists, but more so for the general city newspaper journalists. Your YouTube network could be generating hundreds of thousands of dollars of profit and they won't be impressed, even though it is difficult to carve out any kind of niche within the over saturated market that is YouTube networks.

Worse, many people who are ignorant about new media have their minds made up that running a YouTube channel is not a legit business, so the very idea of running a network of YouTube channels appears outlandishly stupid to them.

It might be tempting to hire a PR company to assist you with scoring press coverage, but I would argue against this. Experience has taught me that most PR companies are more than happy to take your money while delivering no guarantees of coverage. Most PR companies, no matter how notable, are generally useless for actively promoting a business like a YouTube network because they not only lack a core understanding of the business itself, but they also don't have the pull with the limited number of technology journalists who do report on this space.

Most of the time a journalist reports about anything related to YouTube it is because the article was written for them by the internal PR department at the MCN (or even Google themselves), and they simply copy and pasted it onto their blog. It was rather eye-opening for me to meet journalists who write articles about MCNs and discover they know very little about the inner workings of the business.

Worse, I don't think PR helps in channel partner recruiting efforts that much. While it can help establish credibility in the eyes of some creators and strategic partners, it doesn't secure you a deal like having something genuine to offer will. PR is really only useful if you are trying to raise capital from investors.

When I was building Power Up TV the network received hundreds of applications a day from channel owners that wanted to join the network, and it never had any press coverage until I sold the network.

Still, you might try to obtain some press anyway. I encourage you to create an account at MuckRack if you absolutely must try to get press yourself. This service will give you access to a database of journalists and their contact information. This has been the most cost effective way for me to acquire press for my startups without having to hire an outside PR agency.

Attending Conventions

A YouTube network must be part of the creator community in order to attract top tier creators and directly reach the most passionate audiences. The two conventions tailored to YouTubers are,

1. Playlist Live (which operates two annual conventions in Washington DC and Florida)
2. VidCon (an annual convention based in Anaheim, CA).

Now, I realize that with niche focused conventions there is a tendency for varying levels of professionalism in the convention organizers, but my experiences with VidCon and Playlist Live staff have always been very positive. You should not be reluctant to do business with these organizations and they are key to entering the market.

There are also a bunch of conventions focused on specific niches which have cross-over with the YouTube community. For example, gaming conventions like RTX often feature widely subscribed YouTube channel creators who produce gaming-related content.

You might also want to consider attending other kinds of conventions in order to generate relationships with potential sponsors. For example, I have met with digital effects software and video camera equipment manufactures at the annual NAB (National Association of Broadcasters) shows in Las Vegas, Nevada to form sponsorship deals.

Outside of VidCon and Playlist Live, the other conventions you attend will depend greatly on your niche so it's important to make a schedule that is built to prioritize the largest conventions you can attend that will get your brand in front of audiences and potential creator partners to recruit in your network.

The optimal way for recruiting creators or audiences at a convention is to run a contest at your booth and require contest registers to provide you with their email addresses. You can also get info such as if they have a YouTube channel. Later at the office you can send a more detailed survey to those contest entrants who checked the box for YouTube channel creator so you can see if they are a good fit for recruiting to your network.

The bare minimum setup you want for your booth is a step and repeat featuring your brand and some TV monitors for showcasing your video sales pitch that details information about your network. Generally, it's tough to get a reliable internet connection at a convention and I suggest if your display requires a presentation of any kind requiring internet access you might wish to invest into your own 3G hotspot for connecting to the net.

Final Thoughts

I said at the start of this book that what you find here is meant to be an overall primer on the information needed to startup a network, and I feel I have done that. What you ultimately do with this information while building your company is up to you.

If you still have more questions, I wish I could point you in some sort of direction on where to get the answers but alas, I think this book is the only one on the market on how to build a YouTube network.

Considering this, feel free to reach out to me if you have further questions and I will answer them as best I can.

Thanks for reading,

Carey Martell
http://careymartell.com/

Other Books by Carey You May Enjoy

'The Lean Channel: YouTube for Entrepreneurs'

Have you ever wanted to start a business centered around producing YouTube videos? Having trouble convincing viewers to become subscribers? This book serves as a guide for the complete novice instructing in how to get started on your path to becoming a new media sensation and make money.'

http://martellbooks.com/2015/11/30/the-lean-channel-youtube-for-entrepreneurs/

'Agile SCRUM for Film-makers: How to Produce Movies & TV Shows In Half the Time'

If you want to use SCRUM to develop movies and TV shows, 'Agile SCRUM for Film-makers' is the reference guide you've been looking for. Author Carey Martell explains the principles and method of SCRUM, and describes flexible, proven approaches that can help you implement it far more effectively in your production team.

http://martellbooks.com/2015/11/30/agile-scrum-for-film-makers-how-to-produce-movies-tv-shows-in-half-the-time/

'Facebook Marketing: Guide to Strategies That Don't Suck'

In this workbook you will get a crash-course guide in how to setup a branded Facebook Page for your business and grow an audience using both organic (free) strategies. You will also learn how to conduct paid ad campaigns using promoted posts and Facebook Power Editor.

http://martellbooks.com/2015/12/23/facebook-marketing-guide-strategies-dont-suck/

'How to Be a Video Game Journalist: The Reviewer's Guidebook'

Do you like talking about video games? Do you fancy yourself a writer? If yes, you might have want it takes to be a games journalist, but perhaps you aren't sure where to start? The U.S. game industry as a whole was worth USD $10.3 billion, and many of these jobs are held by gaming reporters who form strong relationships with the public relations professionals who work at game publishers.

http://martellbooks.com/2016/03/05/video-game-journalist-reviewers-guidebook/

'How to Start and Run Your Own Video Production Company'

Have you ever wanted your own video production business? Maybe you started out with a plan which quickly evaporated because it seemed too hard? Perhaps there appeared to be insurmountable difficulties involved? Maybe you just didn't think you were getting the right advice? Not anymore. In 'How to Start and Run Your Own Video Production Company,' you will learn every aspect of the trade, from the initial setup to seeing the orders roll in and keeping customers happy.

http://martellbooks.com/2016/02/29/start-run-video-production-company/

'Ultimate Instagram Book: How to Growth Hack 1,000 Likes in 90 Days'

Are you frustrated with the current number of Instagram followers you have? Do you want to know about the fastest, easiest and most surefire way to gain a stupendous number of followers quickly? Want to find out what hash tags your competitors are using? In this book, digital media expert Carey Martell provides you all the necessary steps, tips, and tricks you need to know, from the moment you register for your Instagram account to the stage of increasing user engagement and action to generate sales. Whether you're a startup entrepreneur or a corporate marketer, this book will become a valuable resource.

http://martellbooks.com/2015/12/08/ultimate-instagram-book-growth-hack-1000-likes-90-days/

'YouTube Sponsorships: How Creators Like You Can Fund Your Channel'

Each year companies spend $17 Billion on sponsorships. This is an ideal source of funding to tap into for any YouTube creators. However, many video bloggers simply have no idea what a good sponsorship deal is. They do videos for either low or no money that, if they were more knowledgeable, would have earned them six figure deals. Sport athletes and film actors don't do endorsements for free. Why should you?

http://martellbooks.com/2015/11/30/youtube-sponsorships-how-creators-like-you-can-fund-your-channel-2/

www.ingramcontent.com/pod-product-compliance
Lightning Source LLC
Chambersburg PA
CBHW070849070326
40690CB00009B/1757